BODIES

A SHORT GUIDE TO HOW WE'RE DIFFERENT FOR AWESOME KIDS

BY SHAYLA REESE GRIFFIN

 Justice Leaders PRESS

Detroit, MI

BODIES

BE . . .

DIFFERENT

COLORS

different sizes—

BIG

small

-6
-
-5
-
-4
-
-3
-
-2
-
-1

different heights—

short

tall

BODIES

HAVE . . .

different ways we relate

different ways we
learn & create

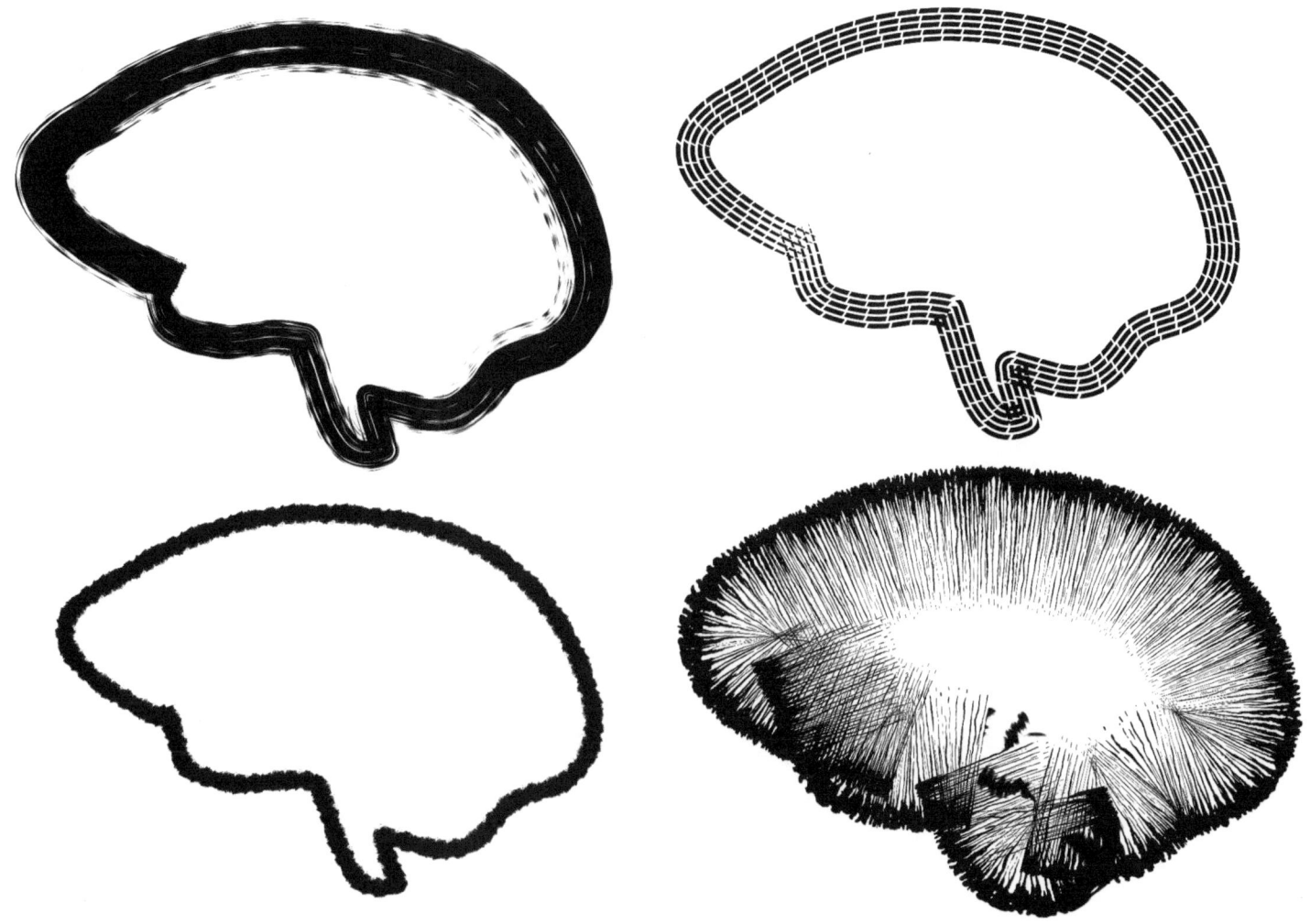

different hair textures–

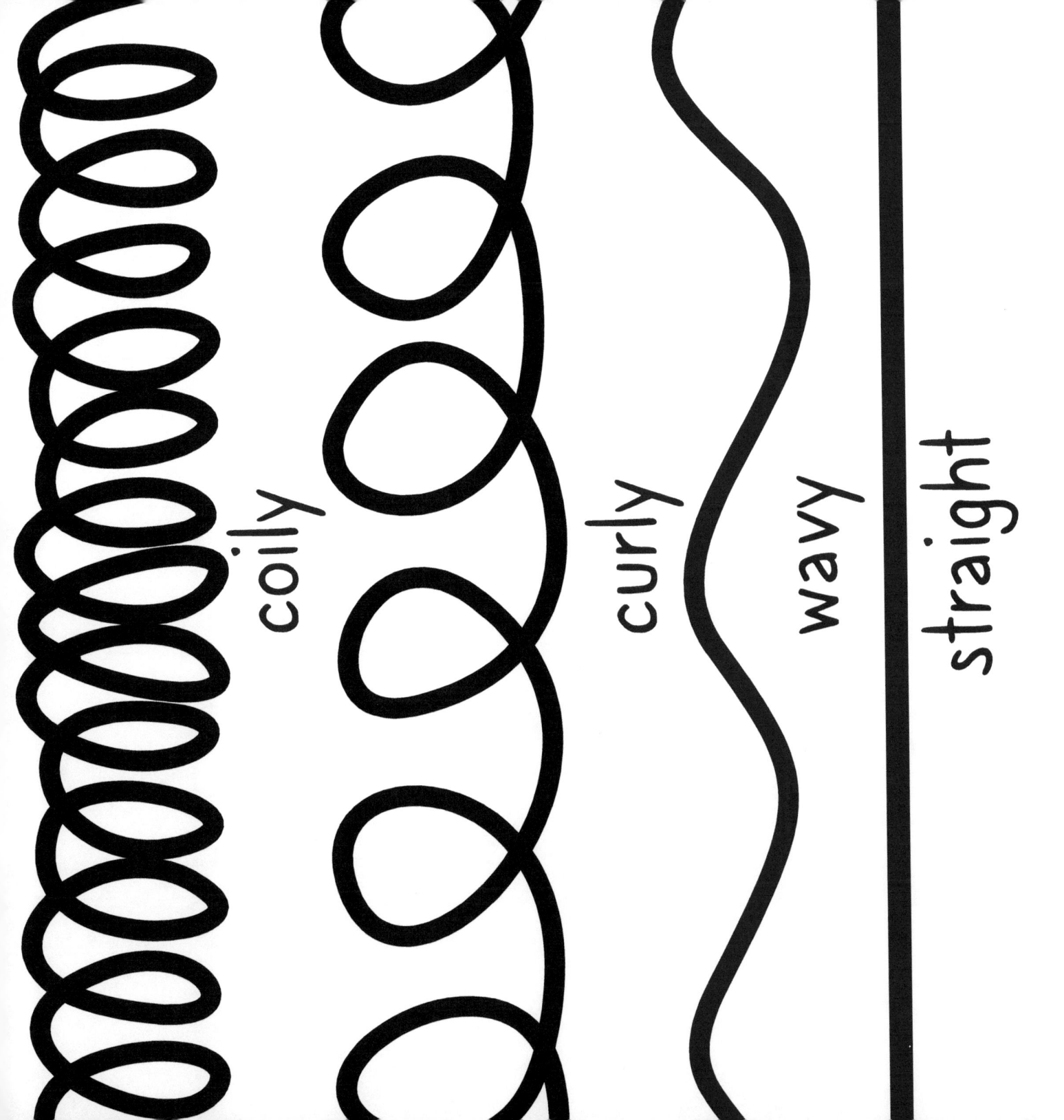

coily

curly

wavy

straight

BODIES

NEED . . .

different things to

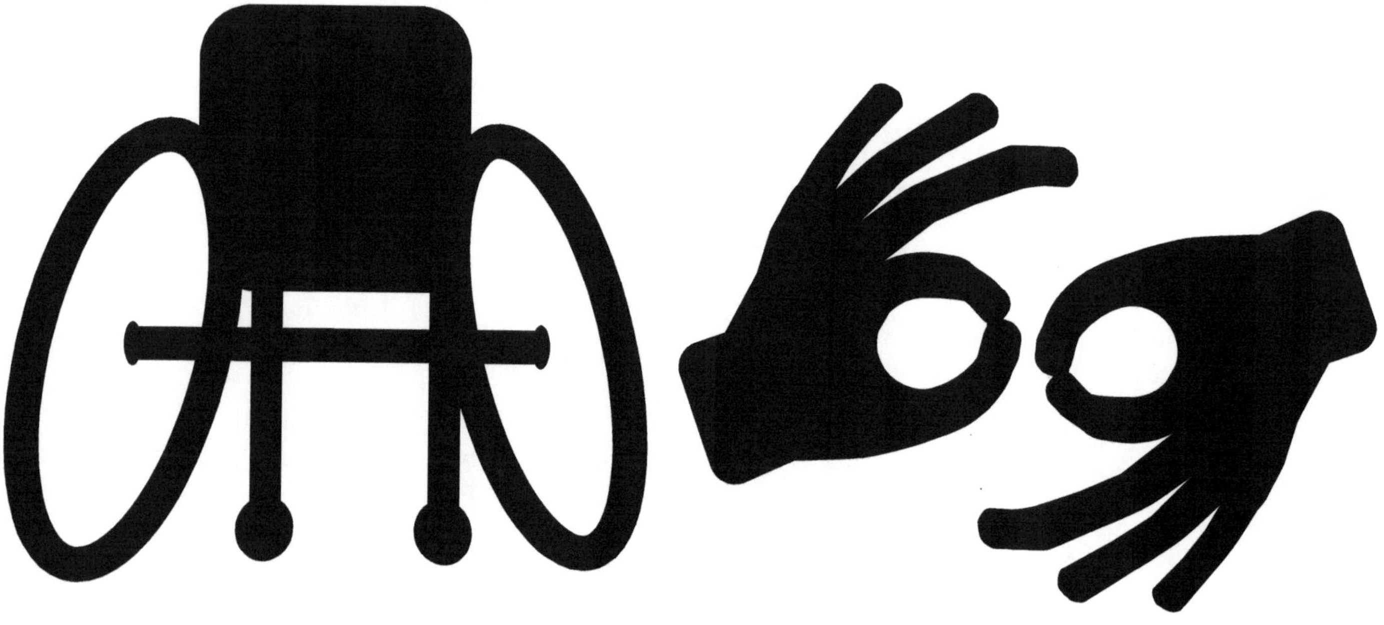

different accommodations

different amounts of sleep

BODIES

LIKE...

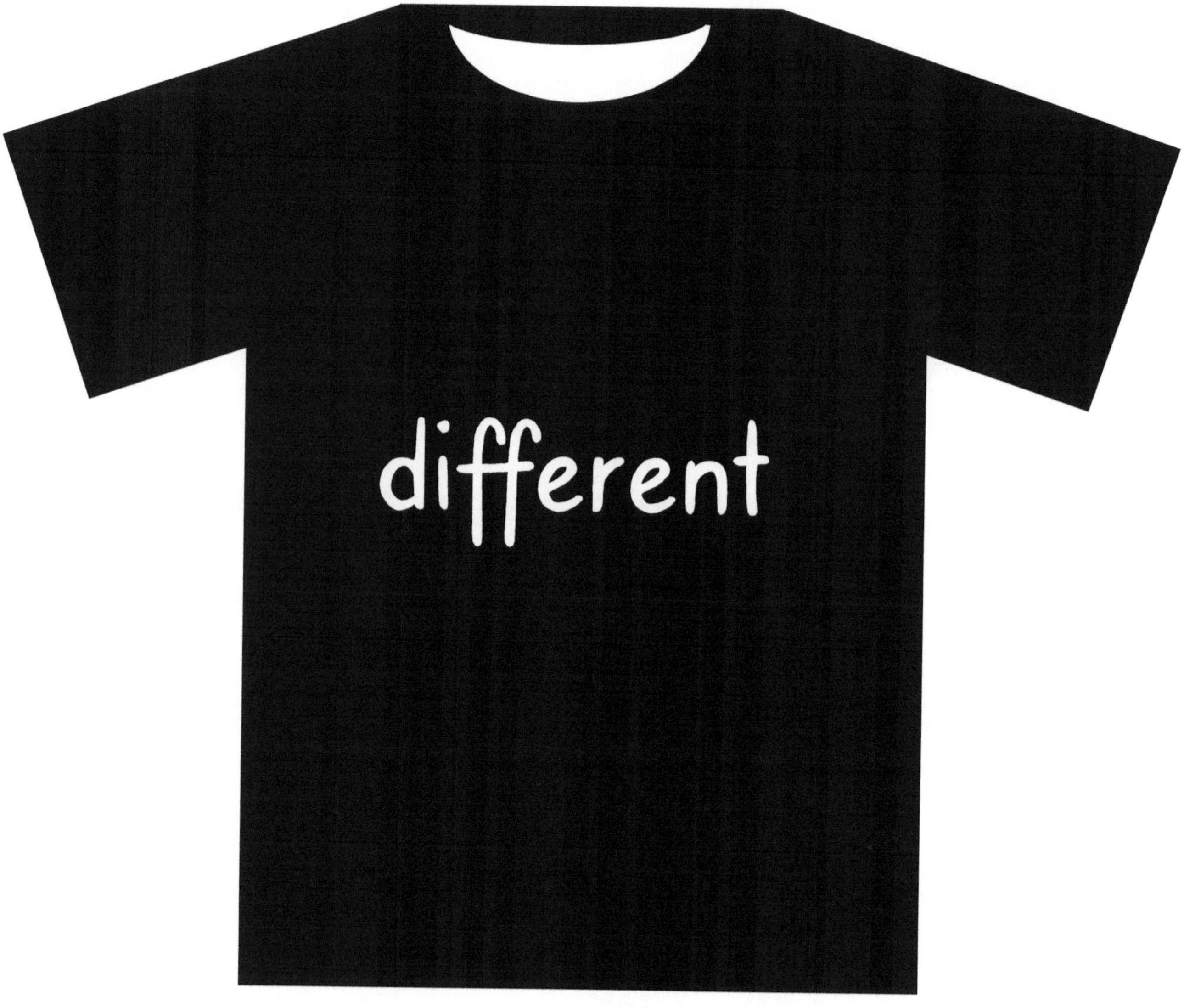
different

weather

different
songs &
jokes

to make
us all
better!

BODIES

FEEL . . .

different emotions—

happy

sad

JEALOUS

MAD

joy
&
delight!

BODIES

PLAY . . .

in all different ways—

s   l   o   w   &

c a u t i o u s

or *speedy* as

light!

BODIES BE

DIFFERENT!

SHAYLA REESE GRIFFIN, PHD, MSW, is co-founder of Justice Leaders Collaborative & Press, which are committed to dismantling oppression, cultivating justice, and nurturing wellbeing through training, consulting, resources, and books. Shayla is the author of *Feel: A Short Guide to A Lot of Emotions for Awesome Kids, Care: A Short Guide to Caring & Sharing for Awesome Kids, Outside: A Short Guide to Connecting with Nature for Awesome Kids, Together: A First Book About Race for Awesome Kids, The Awesome Kids Guide to Race, Those Kids, Our Schools: Race and Reform in An American High School,* and co-author of *Race Dialogues: A Facilitator's Guide to Tackling the Elephant in the Classroom.* She lives with her spouse and three children and gets her best ideas at 3 am.

Published in Detroit, MI in 2025 by Justice Leaders Press www.justiceleaderspress.com
Copyright @ 2025 Shayla Reese Griffin
Written & Illustrated by Shayla Reese Griffin
Edited by David Dobbie, Tori Griffin & Margarette Griffin

Hardcover ISBN: 978-1-969646-95-9
Paperback ISBN: 978-1-969646-96-6
Ebook ISBN: 978-1-969646-97-3
Library of Congress Control Number: 2025919787

If you enjoyed this book and want more from

JUSTICE LEADERS PRESS

please consider supporting our work!

C C C C C C

1. Leave a great rating & review on the website where you purchased this book!
2. Ask your local library or bookstore to carry BODIES: A SHORT GUIDE TO HOW WE'RE DIFFERENT FOR AWESOME KIDS!
3. Share our book with someone in your life!
4. Post about this book on your social media!
5. Place a bulk order for your school or organization! (Contact us at justiceleaderscollaborative@gmail.com for bulk order discounts)
6. Visit www.justiceleaderspress.com for free downloads & to join our mailing list so you'll be the first to know about our upcoming books!

A NOTE ABOUT "BE" In our home, we love using the phrase "bodies *be* different" as a powerful and simple reminder of the many ways we are all unique. I started saying it after having 3 very different babies in just 3 years. Every time we figured out parenting one of them, another one would make clear that "babies be different!" As our kids grew in all different shapes and sizes, with different interests and personalities, our saying evolved into: "*bodies be different*." Using the habitual "be" is common in African American Vernacular English and the alliteration is much more fun to say than "bodies *are* different!"

www.ingramcontent.com/pod-product-compliance
Lightning Source LLC
Chambersburg PA
CBHW041459120626
46547CB00003B/479